The Thing in the Deep

Written by Jan Burchett and Sara Vogler

Illustrated by Carlos Vélez Aguilera

Collins

1 The thing

Abigail and Lee were at the pond.

"What is that deep in the reeds?"
said Abigail. "It seems big!"

"I bet it's just a frog," said Lee.

4

"It's not," said Abigail. "It's this big."

"It must be a fish," said Lee.

"No," said Abigail. "It has a long tail."

"An eel?" said Lee.

"No," said Abigail, grinning. "Its tail has a sting on the end."

2 What is it?

"When it swings its tail, it will sting you," said Abigail.

"It has big, snapping teeth.
It's ... the Creep in the Deep."

"I am NOT waiting to see it," said Lee.

10

"Stop!" said Abigail. "I will sing you the song the Creep sings. You will like it."

Abigail sang.
"I am the Creep
I sleep in the deep
I weep and wail
And thrash my tail
I snap my teeth
And –"

12

13

3 Splash!

All at once, there was a big splash.

14

"What was that thrashing in the weeds?"
said Lee. He was afraid.

The thing was swimming to the bank. It left a trail of green weeds.

Abigail was afraid. "It's the Creep!" she said. "Run!"

The thing sprang out of the pond. It had big teeth and a long tail.

4 Creep in the deep

But Lee did not flee.

The thing was wagging its tail!

"Come back, Abigail," said Lee, grinning. "Come and meet the Creep in the Deep!"

The Creep

After reading

Letters and Sounds: Phases 3 and 4

Word count: 233

Focus phonemes: /sh/ /th/ /ng/ /ai/ /ee/, and adjacent consonants

Common exception words: of, to, the, no, I, all, my, he, she, be, was, you, said, like, come, were, there, when, out, what, once

Curriculum links: PSHE: Keeping safe; Friendships

National Curriculum learning objectives: Reading/word reading: apply phonic knowledge and skills as the route to decode words; read accurately by blending sounds in unfamiliar words containing GPCs that have been taught; read common exception words, noting unusual correspondences between spelling and sound and where these occur in words; Reading/comprehension (KS2): develop positive attitudes to reading and understanding of what they have read by discussing words and phrases that capture the reader's interest and imagination; understand what they read, in books they can read independently, by checking that the text makes sense to them, discussing their understanding and explaining the meaning of words in context; by drawing inferences such as inferring characters' feelings, thoughts and motives from their actions

Developing fluency

- Take turns to read a page, ensuring your child briefly pauses at commas and at the end of each line of the song on page 12.
- Encourage your child to read with expression, using different voices for the children's spoken words.

Phonic practice

- Practise reading words with adjacent consonants:
  creep   splash   trail   sprang
- Challenge your child to read these words with adjacent consonants and the /ng/ sound: swimming   thrashing   creeping   fleeing

Extending vocabulary

- Look at pages 8 and 9. Discuss which phrases rhyme. (*swings, sting*; *Creep in the deep*)
- Together think of more phrases to describe the Creep, focusing on each feature. (e.g. *angry eyes*)
- Challenge your child to think of another name to replace **Creep**. (e.g. *Beast, Spook*)